THE ANCIENT EGYPTIANS

JANE SHUTER

RSVP

RAINTREE
STECK-VAUGHN
PUBLISHERS
A Steck-Vaughn Company

Austin, Texas

www.steck-vaughn.com

HISTORY STARTS HERE!
The Ancient Egyptians
OTHER TITLES IN THE SERIES
The Ancient Greeks • The Ancient Romans
The Aztecs

Published by Raintree Steck-Vaughn Publishers, an imprint of Steck-Vaughn Company

Library of Congress Cataloging-in-Publication Data
Shuter, Jane.
The ancient Egyptians / Jane Shuter
     p.   cm.—(History starts here)
     Includes bibliographical references and index.
     Summary: Examines many different aspects of ancient Egyptian society, including religion, leisure, medicine, art, and technology.
     ISBN 0-7398-1351-X (hard)
     0-7398-2030-3 (soft)
     1. Egypt—Civilization—To 332 B.C.—Juvenile literature.
     [1. Egypt—Civilization—To 332 B.C.]
     I. Title. II. Series.
     DT61.S643   2000
     932'.01—dc21   99-36879

Printed in Italy. Bound in the United States.
1 2 3 4 5 6 7 8 9 0 04 03 02 01 00

Front cover picture: Painted limestone statues of Prince Rahotep and his wife Nofret.
Title page picture: Hunting wildfowl in the marshes along the Nile.

Picture acknowledgments:
Ancient Art and Architecture Collection: 5 (R Sheridan), 6 (Mary Jelliffe), 16 (R Sheridan), 12 (R Sheridan), 20 (R Sheridan), 22 (R Sheridan), 24 (R Sheridan), 26 (Mary Jelliffe); CM Dixon: 8, 9, 10, 11, 13, 14, 17, 18, 21, 23, 24–25, 28; ET Archive: front cover, 1, 19, 27; Tony Stone Images: 29 (Stephen Johnson).
Illustrations: Michael Posen
Cover artwork: Kasia Posen

CONTENTS

THE FIRST EGYPTIANS

The ancient Egyptians lived by the Nile River in Egypt. The Nile River flooded each year, and the mud it left behind was the only soil that crops could grow on. The rest of Egypt was desert. So people lived close to the river.

Ancient Egypt dates from when Upper and Lower Egypt were first ruled by one pharaoh (king). The green shading shows areas where crops could grow.

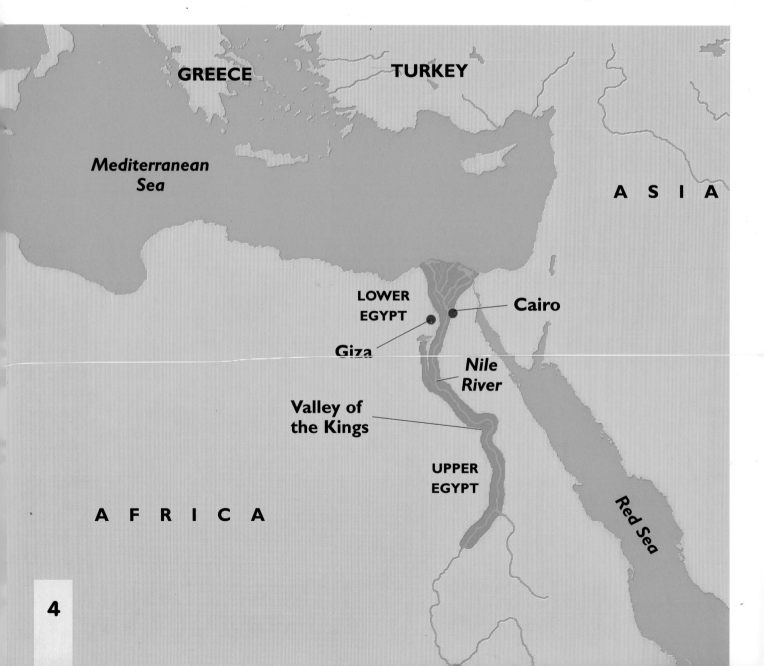

GREECE

TURKEY

Mediterranean
Sea

A S I A

LOWER
EGYPT

Cairo

Giza

Nile
River

Valley of
the Kings

UPPER
EGYPT

A F R I C A

Red Sea

People living in Egypt today still live mostly along the banks of the Nile River. A dam, finished in 1970, was built at Aswan to stop the yearly flooding.

The first ancient Egyptians made their homes along the Nile more than 4,000 years ago. They stayed, living and working there for about 3,000 years. Then other groups of people invaded and took over the country.

RICH AND POOR

A king, called the pharaoh, ruled ancient Egypt. He was the wealthiest and most important person in the country. The least important people were the slaves, who were also the poorest people. Everyone else was in between.

There were rules about who could do each job. Only a few people moved up into more important jobs. Lawbreakers could lose their jobs. They became slaves, or had to do the hardest, worst paid work.

These prisoners have their hands tied behind their backs. They are shown being taken to Egypt where they will become slaves.

This picture shows the different people in Egyptian society. The most important person, the pharaoh, is at the top. The least important people, slaves, are at the bottom.

PHARAOH

Nobles   **Governors**   **High priests**

Craftworkers   **Scribes**   **Artists**   **Priests and priestesses**

Farmers   **Builders**   **Record-keepers**   **Temple workers**   **Fishermen**

Slaves and lawbreakers

HOUSES AND HOMES

Everyone in ancient Egypt lived in homes built from mud bricks—even the pharaoh. Homes had small windows and air vents in the roof, to keep the heat out. Important people had large, beautifully decorated homes.

The white paint on the outside of this house reflected the heat away from the house.

WHAT'S INSIDE?

Ancient Egyptian houses had white inside walls. Poor people decorated their walls with bands of color and simple patterns. Rich people had decorations with complex designs. Homes had very little furniture. Ordinary houses had a mud-brick shelf instead of beds, one or two chairs, and just a few low tables.

Important people had gardens, with pools —cool, shady places to sit in hot weather. Poorer people had small yards or flat roofs where they could relax. They had coverings or climbing plants grown over a frame for shade.

The trees around the pool in a rich family's garden gave shade and fruit to eat.

FAMILY LIFE

The ancient Egyptians thought family life was very important. A marriage began when a couple set up home together. The most important job for women was having children and running the home. But many women, especially in poorer families, had to work as well.

This wooden model shows a woman making bread. Much of the cooking and food preparation was done on the floor in Egyptian homes.

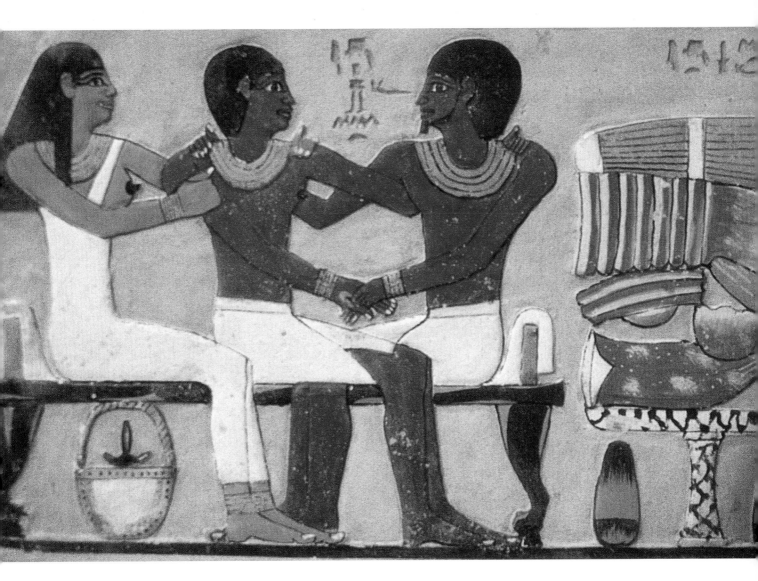

Here a man sits with his wife and son. Men who owned their own homes were expected to look after other family members.

Women were allowed to own their own homes. But they were not allowed to do some jobs, such as helping to rule the country. Men did all the washing because it was done in the Nile River. The river was full of crocodiles.

CHILLDREN

The top of this box is a board for a race game. Underneath is a drawer to keep the playing pieces safe.

Babies and small children played with balls and dolls, just as they do now. Their parents or servants (if they came from a rich family) played with them and told them stories. But as soon as they could, they did simple jobs in the home, the workshop, or the fields. Children were expected to work.

CHILDREN'S NAMES

Parents often named their children after a god or goddess. They expected that a child called She Is Named After Mut would be protected by the goddess Mut. Other parents gave their children names that showed what they wanted the child to be like, such as Happy or Clever.

Wealthy Egyptians wanted their children to be blessed by the gods. Here Akhenaton and Nefertiti are showing their daughters to the sun god Aton.

Only boys training for certain jobs were taught to read and write. Others learned the same trade as their fathers. Some girls, especially in rich families, were taught simple reading and writing at home.

CLOTHES

Clothes in ancient Egypt were mostly made from linen. Rich and poor people wore clothes that were nearly alike. But rich people wore finer cloth, bleached white. Children often wore nothing at all.

Men and women shaved their heads or had very short hair. They wore wigs to dress up. Rich people had wigs made from human hair. Poor people wore wigs made from wool or vegetable fiber. Children's hair was shaved or short. They kept one long plait at the side as a mark of childhood.

Egyptian men wore jewelry like this pectoral—a big necklace that was worn on the chest. It shows a pharaoh between two gods.

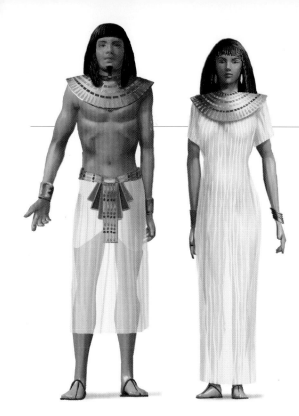

Rich people wore fine clothes, jewelry, makeup, and wigs. They did so because they did not need to work.

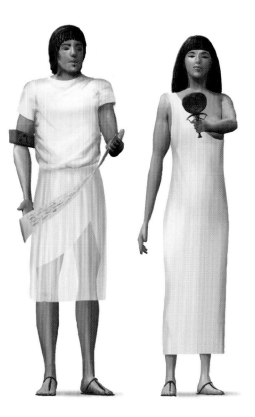

Ordinary people wore clothes made from thicker cloth. They did not wear jewelry while working.

Poor workers needed clothes they could move easily in. The thick linen they used was quite scratchy, but it did not wear out quickly.

FARMING AND TRADE

Every year the Nile River flooded in July. It left mud behind when it went down in October. The mud was the only soil rich enough to grow crops. So farmers worked from November to June, growing enough to feed everyone all year. While the land was flooded, they did other work.

These farmers are going to hit the cut grain to separate it from the stalks. This is known as threshing.

This wooden model of a grain store has real ancient Egyptian grain in it. Grain was ground into flour by crushing it into powder.

Egyptian workers made paper, jewelry, pottery, and cloth. They made sandals and baskets. The ancient Egyptians traded mostly with one another at markets in the towns. They needed to trade with other countries only when their farmers grew too little grain to feed everyone.

FOOD AND DRINK

The most important crop the ancient Egyptians grew was grain. They used grain to make the bread and beer that everyone ate and drank every day. They also ate a lot of vegetables, mostly onions, leeks, cabbage, lettuce, and cucumbers.

Feasts were a way of marking special days, happy or sad. This carving shows a funeral feast.

Poor people did not eat meat very often or even fish from the river. Rich people ate beef, lamb and goat, ducks and geese, and all kinds of fish. Owning animals was a sign of how rich a person was. As well as eating farm animals, people hunted wild animals for sport and food.

This wall painting shows a rich man, Nebamun, hunting in the marshes. With him are his wife, daughter, and specially trained hunting cat.

19

GODS AND TEMPLES

The ancient Egyptians believed in many gods and goddesses. They believed these beings controlled everything—from the sun coming up in the morning to crops growing well. They prayed to their gods at home. And they prayed in temples, where statues of the gods were cared for.

The ancient Egyptians also believed that magic could keep away bad luck or evil spirits. And they thought it could help cure the sick. Doctors often said magic prayers when giving a patient medicine.

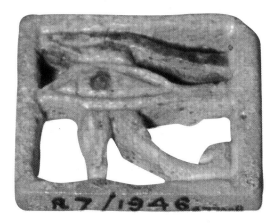

People wore amulets, magic ornaments they believed would keep them from being sick or hurt. These amulets show the eye of the god Horus.

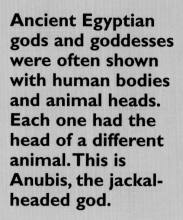

Ancient Egyptian gods and goddesses were often shown with human bodies and animal heads. Each one had the head of a different animal. This is Anubis, the jackal-headed god.

MUMMIES

The ancient Egyptians believed in life after death. So they preserved the bodies of the dead for when they went to the afterlife. They took out the soft parts that would rot and covered the body in salt. It drew out the fluid. They then wrapped the body in long strips of finely woven linen cloth.

This mummy case is decorated with picture writing, called hieroglyphs.

TOO CLEVER?

Maybe the long, difficult ancient Egyptian mummifying process was too clever. Earlier mummies were buried in hot desert sands that soaked up their body fluids. They were preserved just as well!

The soft parts, such as the heart, were taken out of the body. They were preserved in four jars, called canopic jars. Here are two canopic jars.

When prepared, mummies were put into mummy cases made in the shape of a person. The dead were then buried with food, clothes, and makeup. There were also models of things they would need in the next life (such as boats).

THE PYRAMIDS

Most ancient Egyptians were buried in tombs cut into rock or straight into desert sand. But for about 1,000 years, some pharaohs were buried in the most famous ancient Egyptian buildings—pyramids.

Imhotep was a famous Egyptian architect. He designed one of the most famous Egyptian pyramids, at Saqqara.

Pyramids were built from thousands of heavy stone blocks, cut by hand. They were pulled on rollers and put into place by workmen. It was a slow, hard job. The pharaoh's tomb was usually underground. Only a few rooms were above ground.

The tallest of the pyramids at Giza is more than 480 ft. (147 m) high. It was built from more than 2 million stone blocks.

CHEAT!

The biggest pyramid at Giza is the Great Pyramid, at the back of the picture. It was built by the pharaoh Khufu, who ruled from about 2589 B.C. to 2566 B.C. Khufu's son Khafre had the pyramid in the middle built on higher ground. This meant it looked as though it was the biggest.

PAINTING AND WRITING

We know a lot about the ancient Egyptians. We learn by studying the beautiful paintings on the walls of their tombs. Some paintings show people who have died doing ordinary things, such as working, in the afterlife.

Sennedjem and his wife farm in the afterlife, in their best clothes—looking perfect. This is from the wall of his tomb. In real life they would not have farmed at all.

There are hieroglyphs around the painting of the artist Maie and his wife. They tell about things that happened in his life.

The ancient Egyptians used two kinds of writing. Hieroglyphs, the difficult picture writing, were used for important papers and on the walls of tombs and temples. They used a simple form of this for everyday writing.

THE END OF ANCIENT EGYPT

This ancient Egyptian water clock measures 24 hours to every day, just as our clocks do.

The ancient Egyptians were very powerful for about 3,000 years. There were times when other countries tried to take over, but these did not last. However, in 30 B.C. Egypt was swallowed up by the Roman Empire. The ancient Egyptian way of life came to an end.

People are still interested in the ancient Egyptians. Ordinary people visit Egypt and read books about the ancient Egyptians. Archaeologists are still finding their temples, towns, and tombs. Some things that we still use today were invented by the ancient Egyptians. They were the first people to have a year of 365 days divided into 12 months. They also invented clocks.

People still marvel at the Egyptian pyramids and copy the design. This modern glass pyramid is at the Louvre, a museum in Paris.

IMPORTANT DATES

All the dates in this list are "B.C." dates. This stands for "Before Christ." B.C. dates are counted back from the year 0, which is the year we say Jesus Christ was born. Some dates have the letter *c.* in front of them. This stands for *circa*, which means "about." These dates are guesses, because nobody knows what the exact date is.

c. 12,000 People began to settle down to live and grow crops along the banks of the Nile River for the first time.

c. 6000 People began to live in bigger groups and farm and keep animals together. They started to make things, like pottery and tools.

c. 3500 People in Lower and Upper Egypt had found out about one another, by sailing up the river. They began to trade things.

c. 3100 Upper and Lower Egypt were joined together under one pharaoh for the first time.

c. 3000 From this time on people began to write things down and keep lists and official letters.

c. 2686–2181 OLD KINGDOM. All of Egypt was ruled by one pharaoh.

c. 2650–2400 The ancient Egyptians built pyramids to bury their pharaohs in.

c. 2181–2055 Egypt was no longer ruled by one pharaoh. Egyptian rulers in different parts of the country often fought each other.

c. 2055–1650 MIDDLE KINGDOM. All of Egypt was ruled by one pharaoh again.

c. 2000 The pharaoh Amenemhet I began a system of the pharaoh choosing who would rule after him, and ruling with that person for several years before he died. As the country became more settled, Egypt began trading regularly with other countries. More towns were built along the river, and more temples. Now not just pharaohs were mummified and buried in tombs with belongings. More and more people were buried this way.

c. 1550–1069 NEW KINGDOM. All of Egypt was ruled by one pharaoh again.

c. 1550 Pharaohs and other important people were buried in tombs in the rock in the Valley of the Kings and in nearby valleys.

c. 1069–747 Egypt was no longer ruled by one pharaoh.

747–30 LATE PERIOD. All of Egypt was ruled by one pharaoh. The Persians and then the Greeks ruled Egypt. In 30 B.C. it was taken over by the Romans.

GLOSSARY

Air vents Holes made in a building that let air into it and allow air to move around. Air vents are made to let air in, but not rain, dust, or leaves.

Bleached Things are bleached, made white, by soaking them in a weak acid.

Desert Land where little or no rain falls, so the soil is too dry to grow things.

Family members Everyone who belongs to a family, not just parents and children.

Grain A seed, related to grass, that you can eat.

Linen Cloth made from the stems of the flax plant.

Mud brick Building bricks were made from mud that was hardened by drying it in the sun.

Mummify To keep dead bodies from rotting by covering them with special salt.

Pharaoh A king of ancient Egypt.

Slaves People who can be bought and sold as if they are possessions, and who have to work for whoever owns them.

Temples Homes for the gods, where priests go to pray to the gods.

Trade To sell or swap something you do not need in return for something you want.

Weavers People who make cloth by weaving threads under and over each other and pushing the threads so close together that you cannot see through.

BOOKS TO READ

Broida, Marian. *Ancient Egyptians and Their Neighbors*. Chicago: Chicago Review Press, 1999.

Crosher, Judith. *Technology in the Time of Ancient Egypt* (Technology in the Time of). Austin, TX: Raintree Steck-Vaughn, 1998.

Macdonald, Fiona. *The World in the Time of Tutankhamen*. Parsippany, NJ: Dillon Press, 1997.

Martell, Hazel Mary. *The Great Pyramid*. (Great Buildings.) Austin, TX: Raintree Steck-Vaughn, 1998.

Rees, Rosemary. *Ancient Egyptians* (Understanding People in the Past). Portsmouth, NH: Heinemann, 1997.

INDEX